You're Not Tha...

Bir Krishna Swami

Cover Painting and Illustrations
by
Madhava-priya devi dasi

© 1993 Iskcon of North Carolina, Inc.
All Rights Reserved
Printed in the United States of America
ISBN 0-944969-01-1

Readers interested in the subject matter of this book are invited to correspond with the author at the following address:

Bir Krishna Swami
P.O. Box 897
Hillsborough, N.C. 27278

*Dedicated to the memory of
Shri Bapubhai Raghunathji Desai
by his son
Prakash B. Desai*

Explanation of the cover picture

You're not that body!

Five thousand years ago Krishna, the Supreme Personality of Godhead, spoke the *Bhagavad-gita* (the **Song of God**) which contains information about God, the living entities, karma (action and reaction in this world), time, and the material energy.

The *Bhagavad-gita* is one of the *Vedic* literatures. The word veda (from which the word *Vedic* comes) means knowledge. The *Vedic* literatures deal with spiritual and material subject matters. The knowledge they contain is perfect, because of its perfect source--God, or God's devotees in disciplic succession from God.

The *Bhagavad-gita* teaches us that the soul is unbreakable, unchangeable, insoluble, everlasting, immovable, and neither burnt nor dried.[1] The *Vedic* literatures inform us that there are many eternal souls of whom the chief is Krishna, Who is maintaining all of the other souls.[2]

The *Bhagavad-gita* explains that the body, which we (who are souls) identify ourselves with in the material world, is simply a machine. It is, of course, a very complex, wonderful machine. Nonetheless, it is still a machine.[3]

In the way that one drives a car, the soul is driving the body. Unfortunately the soul thinks that it is the body, so the characteristics that pertain to a particular body are thought by the soul to be its characteristics. For example: if the body is white, has a gigantic nose, is female, and is born in the United States; the soul thinks that

1

it is an American white woman that needs a nose job.

Because of the soul's identification with the characteristics of the body, he (the soul) identifies others according to their machine-body characteristics, and forms alliances and animosities accordingly. Thus he develops family attachment, racism, nationalism and even specism; which are all manifestations of the same disease (misidentification of the self with the body). When the soul becomes Krishna conscious he no longer distinguishes between living entities because of the differences in the bodily encagement; therefore he sees the true equality of all beings.

The soul is situated along with God (the Supersoul) in the heart of this machine. The soul is driving this machine according to his desires. The Supersoul is observing the soul's actions, and waiting patiently for the soul to become frustrated in its attempts to enjoy through manipulating the machine-body.

When the soul decides that its attempts at enjoyment have been futile and that all future endeavors will miserably fail, he may decide to seek out God. At this point Krishna sends His representative in the form of the spiritual master to guide the soul on its spiritual path. The soul, being covered by the material energy, is not capable of perceiving the existence and direction of the Supersoul who is situated next to him in the heart. Therefore the Supersoul directs His external representative (the spiritual master) to help the sincere searcher.

1. Bhagavad-gita 2.24
2. Katha Upanisad 2.2.13
3. Bhagavad-gita 18.61

Lord Caitanya

The *Vedas* call the present age the "Age of *Kali*"-the age of quarrel. This age began approximately 5,000 years ago. In this age people are less fortunate, less intelligent, shorter lived, have shorter memories, and have weaker bodies. Good qualities such as sympathy for others, education, truthfulness, cleanliness, forgiveness, and mercy are quickly disappearing. Society is beset with cheating, diplomacy, and violence. The so-called leaders of society are encouraging intoxication, illicit sex, gambling, and meat eating, which are considered the principles of irreligiousity.

There is one good quality in this age. That is, simply by chanting the Lord's names, one can escape the miseries of this age, and go back to the kingdom of God at the end of life.[1]

Krishna incarnates in every age to preach the religious practice that is applicable for that particular age. In other ages Krishna taught meditational yoga, or temple worship, or sacrifice.

Krishna appeared about 500 years ago as Lord Caitanya. This advent was predicted in the *Vedic* literatures more than 5,000 years ago. Lord Caitanya taught the religious practice recommended for this age, Sankirtana, the congregational chanting of the Lord's names: **Hare Krishna Hare Krishna Krishna Krishna Hare Hare Hare Rama Hare Rama Rama Rama Hare Hare**.

Devotees of the Krishna consciousness movement engage in the chanting of the Lord's names in public, distributing transcendental literatures (which encourage others to chant), and performing personal meditation on the Lord's names (called *Japa*).

1. Srimad-Bhagavatam 12.3.51

Reincarnation

Reincarnation means that the soul is changing bodies. This change of bodies occurs not only at death, but throughout life; from boyhood to youth to old age, then to a baby's body.[1] These moment by moment changes are too small for the person to be aware of, but when we consider greater amounts of time, then the change of bodies is obvious. The change of body known as death is the most apparent.

The *Bhagavad-gita* compares the change of body at the time of death to a person discarding old and useless clothes, and putting on new garments.[2] Regardless of whatever plans and adjustments we make, our body eventually wears out, and we are obliged to accept a new one.

Although everyone must die, still we are making plans as though death was not certain. Saints have described this as the most amazing thing in this world. That is, even though we see that everyone is dying and getting old, we think that it will not happen to us, and we neglect the real purpose of human life: self-realization. One must inquire as to what happens at the time of death.

Although one may have the body of a man in this life, the soul may take the body of a woman in the next. One may have an oriental body in one birth, a western body in the next; or one may take birth in an animal or insect species as a result of one's activities and desires in this life. It is important to understand how the soul transmigrates from one body to the next.

1. Bhagavad-gita 2.13
2. Bhagavad-gita 2.22

How is Our Next Body Determined?

There are two factors that determine which body we shall obtain in the next birth. The first is our karma--the reactions to our good and bad activities that were performed in this life and in previous lives. The second factor is our desire to enjoy particular sense objects.

The example of a man purchasing a car is appropriate in this regard. He has a desire to enjoy in a particular way with his car, and he also has a certain amount of money to spend. He takes both factors into account to determine which model to purchase.

Krishna tells us that the state of consciousness that we have upon leaving the present body determines the type of body that we will have in the next birth.[1] This is our "final exam" which we should study for throughout this life by cultivating remembrance of Krishna. One may think that at the time of death he will suddenly make up for the rest of his life by "getting religion." However, things don't work that way. The thoughts, desires and attachments that one has cultivated throughout his life will be reflected in those final moments. There is no way to cheat on this "exam."

As far as activities are concerned, we should only perform activities that carry no *karmic* weight (technically called "*akarmic*" activities), so that we will not have to return to this world either to receive bad or good results. Then we will return to the spiritual abode of the Lord.

1. Bhagavad-gita 8.6

8

Tendencies of Conditioned Souls

We are part and parcels of God, pure spiritual entities by nature, but due to contact with the material energy we become covered by ignorance.

Because of this covering, we display faults in our character. Four types of faults are especially prominent: 1. The tendency to make mistakes, 2. The tendency to be illusioned, 3. Having imperfect senses, and 4. The propensity to cheat. Every conditioned soul (contaminated by material consciousness) is subject to these four defects. Therefore the conditioned soul is not able to distinguish between matter and spirit, nor give adequate spiritual guidance to others.

In order to progress spiritually, we must take guidance from persons who are free from these four defects. God and His pure devotees are free from these defects. Religious principles can only be given by God. His pure devotees simply repeat these principles. They do not speculate as do mundane theologians, whose presentations are, at best, pseudo spirituality.

If one tries to manufacture his own religious process, pick and choose practices as he likes, or follow a spiritual guide who is not a pure devotee of God then he will be victimized by these four defects. Even a bonafide spiritual process, if interpreted by someone who is not pure, will be contaminated and not yield spiritual fruit. Only by strictly following the instructions of God, as repeated by His pure devotee can one be freed of these four faults.

The Post-Graduate Study of God

There is one God. All bonafide religious scriptures teach of the same God and stress the importance of loving Him. Religion, in fact, means to come to the stage of loving God without any personal self-centered motivation.

Because of the different circumstances in which God consciousness is taught, there are different grades of information given to the spiritual aspirants. For example, if people are very degraded and engaged in gross sinful practices, it may be necessary to stress sub-religious principles that must be followed just to bring them to the human platform. One may preach "Thou shalt not kill" or "Do not commit adultery" or "Honor your father and mother".

In this way, the saints preach according to time, place and circumstance, taking into account what each group of persons needs in order to advance to the next stage of God-consciousness. In the Krishna consciousness movement, spiritual aspirants are instructed in the four regulative principles: 1. No meat, fish or eggs, 2. No illicit sex, 3. No gambling, and 4. No intoxication. If someone does not follow these principles, he can never understand God.

The higher principles taught in the *Vedic* literatures, such as the nature of God, the nature of pure love of God, the nature of the spiritual world and activities there, are considered the post-graduate study of God-consciousness. Srila Prabhupada's books deal with this most exalted science.

Methods of Obtaining Knowledge

There are three basic methods of obtaining knowledge, two of which are faulty, and one which is faultless when properly applied. The two faulty methods are: 1. Direct perception, and 2. Induction (making general conclusions from limited experience). The faultless method is the descending process by which one hears from the proper authority who is faultless (Krishna or His pure devotees).

The two faulty methods are known as the "ascending process." "Ascending" means to go up. So one who follows these processes is trying to understand God or Truth with his limited faulty faculties. We see the adherents of these methods changing their theories constantly. They are not sure of anything.

In Krishna consciousness we hear Krishna's opinion which is perfect, because He is omniscient; that is, there is nothing unknown to Him. His words are always perfect and true. There is no need of a new opinion every 5 minutes. Krishna's devotees who are in the disciplic succession simply repeat His words and therefore what they speak is also perfect.

Srila Prabhupada gave the example of a small boy who asks his father what is the name of the object into which his father is speaking. His father replies, "microphone." The boy repeats. Even though the boy may not have complete understanding, because he is repeating what is true, his words are true.

Revelation, not speculation, is the only way one can understand God. Krishna wants us to know Him, so He reveals Himself through the scriptures and His pure devotees.

The Spiritual Master

The *Vedas* tell us that if one wants to make advancement in spiritual life it is imperative to accept a spiritual master.[1] In any discipline we need a teacher. Book learning is not sufficient. For example, a surgeon must study under an expert experienced surgeon. He cannot confine his learning to books. One who does not accept a bonafide spiritual master as his guide is sure to be bewildered in his attempts at self-realization.

One must be extremely careful in choosing a spiritual master, as there are many pretenders who simply wish to cheat innocent persons.

There are standards mentioned in the *Vedic* literature that one should use when picking one's eternal guide: 1. The spiritual master must come in an unbroken chain of disciplic succession from God Himself, 2. The spiritual master must be a perfect disciple of his spiritual master; a first class servant rendering humble service, 3. The spiritual master must be fixed in the regulative principles and practices of Krishna consciousness, never falling down, 4. The spiritual master must have heard nicely from his spiritual master so that he is simply repeating in his own words the teachings given to him.

The spiritual master teaches by example as well as precept. By observing his behavior, the prospective disciple can verify that the spiritual master is not deviating from the teachings that he received from his own spiritual master and is, in turn, passing along to his disciples. In this way, the disciple can understand how to apply the teachings to his own life.

1. Mundaka Upanisad 1.2.12

The Disciplic Succession

In order to make progress in spiritual life the *Vedas* enjoin that one must accept a spiritual master in disciplic succession from God Himself.[1] In this way, the knowledge revealed directly by God is carefully passed down without change from spiritual master to disciple.

The members of the Krishna consciousness movement are in the *Brahma-Madhva Gaudiya* disciplic succession. This succession originated with Lord *Brahma,* the first created being in this universe. He was instructed directly by the Supreme Lord from within the heart. Lord *Brahma's* disciple was *Narada Muni. Narada Muni's* disciple was *Srila Vyasadeva.* The disciplic succession was carried forward to Lord Caitanya, who, although He is Krishna Himself, accepted a spiritual master in this line to set an example. Lord Caitanya's direct disciples were the Six *Goswamis* of Vrindavana, who carried out the tradition by initiating disciples of their own and writing volumes of books about the Supreme Personality of Godhead. In the modern age we have Srila Bhaktivinoda Thakura, Srila Gaura-kisora das Babaji Maharaja, Srila Bhaktisiddhanta Sarasvati Thakura, and Srila Prabhupada; the founder-acharya of the International Society for Krishna Consciousness.

Srila Prabhupada empowered his disciples to carry out this most sacred tradition. The disciplic succession is therefore continuing.

1. Mundaka Upanisad 1.2.17

Who is Srila Prabhupada?

Srila Prabhupada, the founder-acharya of the International Society for Krishna Consciousness, is a *nitya-siddha* devotee of Lord Krishna. This means that he has always been perfect in Krishna consciousness. It is not that he attained that state at some point in time. He descended from the spiritual world at the request of the Supreme Lord to preach Krishna consciousness.

Srila Prabhupada, translated, commented on, and published many books. Through these books knowledge of Krishna consciousness has been spread throughout the world. Srila Prabhupada informed us that he is present in his books. He stated that the publication of his books was his most important preaching activity. Lord Krishna can be found in every page, and, in fact, every word of his books. Anyone who reads or even respects his books will become a devotee of Lord Krishna.

While he was here with us on this planet, he stressed the distribution of his books and encouraged his disciples to increase the numbers of books distributed year by year. He told them that he would live forever in his books. Hundreds of millions of his books have been distributed to date.

Srila Prabhupada stated that his books are the law books for the Krishna consciousness movement, and, one day, would be the law books for all human society.

When Krishna Comes to this World

In the *Bhagavad-gita* Krishna states that He comes to this world whenever there is a rise in irreligion and a decline in religion.[1] He comes to reestablish religious principles, annihilate the miscreants, and protect the devotees.[2]

By the phrase "rise in irreligion," Krishna indicates that irreligious activities such as meat eating, illicit sex, intoxication, gambling, and Godlessness in general are widespread. In the modern age, we not only find the majority of the populace performing these irreligious acts, but the government and leaders in general are encouraging irreligion.

One who performs irreligious acts is breaking the laws of God, which are immutable. Modern theologians very enthusiastically declare that religious principles must be changed or adapted to meet the changing conditions in this world. But God does not see things this way. He holds one responsible for breaking His laws regardless of what excuse one may offer, or what theologian one may quote.

In this age of *Kali* (quarrel) Krishna appears as His Holy Names: Hare Krishna Hare Krishna Krishna Krishna Hare Hare, Hare Rama Hare Rama Rama Rama Hare Hare. Simply by worshiping Him by chanting these names, one can attain all spiritual perfection and be freed from the influence of this dark age.

1. Bhagavad-gita 4.7
2. Bhagavad-gita 4.8

The Four Sinners-The Four Saints

In the *Bhagavad-gita* Krishna explains the four types of persons who reject Him, as well as the four types of persons who approach Him.[1]

The types that reject Him are: 1. The man who works like an ass and tries to enjoy like one, forgetting God completely, 2. Someone who is not even civilized enough to think of God, 3. Someone who is caught up in the pursuit of mundane knowledge, and 4. The out and out atheist who is determined never to worship God and attempts to convert others to his view point.

God is approached by those: 1. Desiring relief from distress, 2. Desiring knowledge, 3. Desiring wealth or other material benefits, and 4. Who are inquisitive or curious. Of course these are mixed motives, but ultimately one will be purified of these if one sticks to the spiritual path.

"Pure love of God" means that one simply wants to please God, and one is ready to sacrifice his own happiness to accomplish this end. When one feels this way, he experiences the greatest happiness. Pure love of God is the greatest gift that God can give.

1. Bhagavad-gita 7.16, 7.19

Impersonalism vs. Personalism

Many transcendentalists attempt to escape the miserable conditions of this world by approaching God. Unfortunately, many of them think that the highest realization of God is His energy. Thus, they realize the eternal aspect of the Lord, but never get to enjoy the knowledge and bliss that accompany personal realization.

Impersonalists often speak of God as "The Light" or "The Force", but these (the light and the force) are His energies. God is a person, the controller and proprietor of these energies, and when the impersonalists seek to merge with His energies, they miss the joy of a personal relationship with Him. The impersonalist thinks that by losing his personality in "oneness" with God he will find relief from suffering; but the devotee knows that the soul's individual identity is never lost. By having a spiritual relationship with the Lord, the individual soul will discover, and be able to express his real personality, experience complete satisfaction, and be free from all suffering.

The soul is by nature active and pleasure seeking; therefore, in the unnatural situation of impersonal realization, the soul is dissatisfied, and again falls down to this world, attempting to enjoy the material variety, being unaware of the spiritual variety that a devotee enjoys in the association of the Personality of Godhead, Krishna.

The sun is the energetic source of the sunshine (the energy). The energetic is comparatively more important than its energy. In the same way the devotees recognize Krishna as the energetic source of all energies. The devotees worship the energetic (Krishna) rather than His energy, and reject the idea of merging into His energy.

Remembrance, Forgetfulness and Knowledge

Krishna, as the Supersoul in everyone's heart, helps one to fulfill one's desires in this world. According to our aspirations, we require to forget some things (such as God if one is an atheist), we require to remember other things, and we need knowledge.[1]

Even the animals have instinctually based behavior that coincides with their desires. This so-called instinct is actually Krishna in the heart helping them to carry out their plans. Krishna knows the aspirations of all living entities.

Krishna does this to give them facility to enjoy all of the varieties in this world. When the soul has finally realized the futility of attempting to enjoy separately from God, he turns to Krishna in the heart.

We have forgotten that we are part and parcels of Krishna, His eternal servants, because we want to pretend to be the "master of all we survey." Krishna, however, sends messengers (saints, sages, preachers) to us to remind us of who we are. Krishna says that to one who seeks Him, serving Him with devotion, He gives knowledge how to approach Him.[2] When someone comes to full Krishna consciousness, He reveals their eternal relationship with Him and removes all ignorance.

1. Bhagavad-gita 15.15
2. Bhagavad-gita 10.10

The Perverted Material World

In the *Bhagavad-gita*, Krishna compares this material realm with a banyan tree that has its roots upwards and branches down.[1] We may think that such a tree does not exist, but we can perceive such a tree as the reflection of an actual tree on the bank of a river.

The root of such a tree, or where the actual tree and the reflected tree join, can be compared to the desire of the individual soul, which is manifest by his utilization of free will. By his free will he may choose to enter into the spiritual realm (actual tree) or the material world (reflected tree).

Just as a reflection is an inverted replica of the original, the relationships in this world are reversed representations of the relationships in the kingdom of God.

The *Vedas* tell us that there are five *rasas*, or relationships, that exist in the transcendental dimension: 1. Passive adoration, 2. Servitude, 3. Friendship, 4. Parental affection, and 5. Conjugal love. The rasas are sometimes flavored by indirect relationships that come and go appropriately according to different situations. All of these relationships have as their focal point Krishna, Who is understood as the enjoyer in every instance, whereas the individual soul is the enjoyed, taking as his only pleasure the satisfaction of the Supreme Soul. This attitude brings complete satisfaction to the soul.

Here in the perverted reflection (material world) the individual soul attempts to be the enjoyer, taking all other entities, the material energy, and even God as the objects of enjoyment. The conditioned soul structures his life in such a way as to maximize this enjoyment, but is continuously frustrated. Ultimately, everything is taken away by the Supreme Lord in the form of time.

1. Bhagavad-gita 15.1

Material Love

What we call "love" in this world is simply the self-centered desire to enjoy the "beloved" object. So our love for something or someone is dependent upon whether or not our senses are being pleased.

For example, people generally love animals such as cats because of the sensual attraction to soft fur, or dogs because of the dog's desire to please the master. But, very few people are interested in embracing a cockroach, because a cockroach is displeasing to our senses. However, a cockroach is a living entity with feelings like any other due to its essential spiritual nature.

When we think that we are experiencing a loving mood with some other creature, we are illusioned because we are unaware of their consciousness which is not "at one" with ours. It is thinking of its own gratification.

When one loves Krishna, one will love all living entities equally and truly, because of the spiritual family relationship that is there. Krishna tells us that we are all His "parts and parcels", His sons and daughters. A devotee of Krishna has no hatred for any living entity, just pure, unselfish love.

A Krishna conscious person is able to properly express this unselfish love and benefit all living entities, because he is aware of their real self-interest. However others, even if they are well-intentioned, can never give any real help to the self--the soul in the body. Material help is temporary. Spiritual help is eternal.

The real self-interest of all living entities is Krishna consciousness.

The Modes of Nature

The *Bhagavad-gita* informs us that all conditioned souls are forced to act helplessly by the impulses born of the modes of material nature.[1] The soul is thinking that he is acting by his own volition but in actuality the modes are shaping the soul's desires and actions.

There are three modes of nature: goodness, passion, and ignorance. According to the specific combination of the three modes that a soul is affected by, he acts accordingly. The three modes combine to provide the impulses for every conceivable type of activity in this world, just as the three primary colors can be combined to yield all the colors of the spectrum.

According to the combination of modes, one is attracted to certain types of eatables. For example, the pig is very enthusiastic to partake of stool (which human beings consider abominable), because the pig loves food in the mode of ignorance. Food in the mode of goodness is sweet, juicy, fattening, and palatable.[2] Food in the mode of passion is too bitter, too sour, too salty, pungent, dry, and hot.[3] Food in the mode of ignorance is decomposed, tasteless, stale, putrid, and unclean (such as meat).[4]

A devotee is only interested in eating food that has been offered to Krishna which purifies his consciousness, and helps him in his spiritual progress.

1. Bhagavad-gita 3.5
2. Bhagavad-gita 17.8
3. Bhagavad-gita 17.9
4. Bhagavad-gita 17.10

Frustration and Material Pleasure

Our nature is spiritual--different from the material body that we are inhabiting. We can never become happy by attempting to satisfy the body. The soul must be satisfied.

Srila Prabhupada gave an example of the "Bird in the Cage" to illustrate this point. If the owner of the bird only pays attention to the cage, polishing it carefully, and neglects the inhabitant of the cage (the bird), the bird will die. In the same way, if we simply pay attention to the body, neglecting its inhabitant (the soul), spiritually we will be as good as dead. Of course, the soul never dies; but he will certainly be very miserable.

Our practical experience is that even when we obtain some object that we think will satisfy our senses, we soon become frustrated because the happiness is not forthcoming. The material world is arranged in such a way that despite all attempts at enjoyment, the conditioned soul is continuously frustrated. Fulfilling the desires of the senses does not bring peace, because even if the senses are temporarily satisfied, they demand newer and newer experiences. They are insatiable. Rather than becoming satisfied, the senses become inflamed by the process of seeking enjoyment.[1] Thus, the living entity alternates between boredom and craving. Because of this frustration we become angry and often end up fighting with others.

Krishna conscious happiness is not like that. It is unlimited, and goes on eternally.

1. Bhagavad-gita 3.39

Three Gates Leading to Hell

The *Bhagavad-gita* describes that there are three gates leading to hell: lust, anger, and greed. These activities cloud the consciousness like a drug and have caused many people to lose their good name, morality, family and health, as well as to grievously harm others. Spiritually, these activities blind a person and make him unable to understand spiritual truth. Falling deeper and deeper into illusion, the soul will have to suffer greatly. One who is sane should give up these three principles.[1] By following the four regulative principles and chanting the Hare Krishna *Maha-Mantra*: **Hare Krishna Hare Krishna Krishna Krishna Hare Hare Hare Rama Hare Rama Rama Rama Hare Hare**, one becomes gradually freed of these unwanted desires.

When Lord Krishna appeared 500 years ago as Lord Caitanya, He compared the process of chanting Hare Krishna to the cleansing of a mirror. The mirror of our mind or consciousness is clouded by the contaminated association that we have had in this world; not only during this lifetime but throughout past lives. The chanting cleanses the mirror of the mind, puts out the fire of material lust, makes our lives auspicious, situates us on the transcendental platform, awakens us to transcendental knowledge, and gives us the pleasure for which we have been hankering.[2]

The chanting of the Lord's names is the most important activity for a devotee. This chanting is the religious practice of this age (*Yuga-dharma*). A devotee should chant incessantly. In order to do this one must cultivate humility.[3]

1. Bhagavad-gita 16.21
2. Sri Sri Siksastaka 1
3. Sri Sri Siksastaka 3

FALSE EGO INTELLIGENCE MIND ether air CHEMICALS cement fire water earth

Krishna's Energies

Krishna, the Supreme Lord, has three types of energies: 1. Material, 2. Spiritual, and 3. Marginal. The material energy is the dull matter that has no consciousness. The spiritual energy is the conscious energy that is devoted to His service. The marginal energy consists of the living entities--individual souls, such as ourselves, that have the choice of either identifying with matter or spirit.

In actuality, the marginal potency (individual spirit souls) is also spiritual. Because of his marginal position, the soul can be illusioned by the material energy, and completely forget his real nature. As soon as the soul associates with the material nature, he becomes conditioned. He tries to enjoy this material world, which is by nature different from him, and consequently he is frustrated in his attempt.

If the spirit soul associates with the spiritual nature through the processes of devotional service: hearing about Krishna, chanting His glories, remembering Him, worshiping Him, serving His lotus feet, offering prayers, carrying out His orders, becoming His friend, and surrendering to Him, the soul will be situated in his constitutional position and enjoy unlimitedly.

The soul is often compared to a small spark that will only continue blazing as long as it remains in the fire. When it is removed from the fire its illumination is quickly extinguished. Similarly, the soul will experience eternity, bliss and knowledge only as long as he remains engaged in Krishna's service. Otherwise, his true nature will be covered.

Krishna is Everywhere

Krishna is in everyone's heart, and, in fact, in every atom of the creation. Nothing exists without Krishna. He appears in His expansion as the Supersoul. In this form, He is guiding us in this world giving us intelligence, remembrance, and forgetfulness; and patiently waiting for us to give up our futile endeavor to enjoy the material world.[1]

The *Vedic* literatures describe that there are two souls in the heart of every entity: God and the individual soul. This is compared to two birds in a tree; one bird is trying to enjoy the fruits of the tree, while the other is observing.[2] When the bird who is trying to enjoy (the individual soul) turns to the observing bird (God), God becomes pleased and sends a spiritual master to the individual soul to guide him on his spiritual path.

Because the conditioned soul is covered with the material energy, he is not capable of perceiving directly the existence and direction of the Supersoul who is situated next to him in the heart; but when the Supersoul sends His external manifestation (the spiritual master) to help the sincere seeker, the soul is able to perceive spiritual reality through the words of the spiritual master. Gradually, as the soul comes to Krishna consciousness, he will be able to perceive Krishna in his heart, as well as in everything around Him.

1. Bhagavad-gita 15.15
2. Svetasvatara Upanisad 4.7

Krishna Is The Reservoir of All Beauty

The *Bhagavad-gita* states that everything comes from Krishna.[1] In the tenth chapter, He says that He is the source of all material and spiritual worlds.[1]

As the Universal Form, Krishna's features are bewildering even to his pure devotees. But, in His original feature with two hands holding a flute, He is unlimitedly attractive. Devotees are interested in worshiping Krishna in His original form.

The source of anything contains all the qualities present in the emanation and more. For example, in our homes we have the benefit of electricity which ultimately comes from a large power station situated miles away. We can understand that the power station's capacity to generate electricity far exceeds the tiny amount that we have access to in our homes. The beauty of Krishna far exceeds anything that is present in His creation.

The attractive features of Krishna have been classified in six different divisions by the great sages. He is 1. All beautiful, possessing perfect bodily characteristics, 2. All knowing, 3. Completely renounced, 4. The strongest person, 5. The most wealthy, and 6. The most famous.

The more we learn about Krishna, His appearance, His qualities, and His personality, the more we will be attracted to Him and our natural love for Him will be awakened.

1. Bhagavad-gita 10.8

Krishna's Body is Spiritual

Krishna is non-different from His body. His body is eternal, full of bliss, and knowledge.[1] He never changes His body, but in His selfsame body appears in different ways, according to His desires, in His various incarnations.[2] This is the same as a dramatic artist who can expertly assume different roles according to the scripts which he is called upon to perform. It is stated in the Vedic literatures, that when we see God in His original manifestation, He is known as Krishna--the all attractive Personality of Godhead.

In His various manifestations in this world, Krishna establishes religious principles, annihilates miscreants, and helps His devotees.[2] At the same time, He exhibits these activities to attract people who have no information about God other than their faulty speculation or the speculations of others such as theologians. When people see or hear about Krishna's wonderful activities, they become attracted to Him, and become interested in spiritual life.

Krishna also enjoys acting in many different ways. God is not impersonal. He has desires like ourselves, but His desires are not fraught with the impurities that contaminate ours. He enjoys dancing, playing, singing, fighting, and all the activities that we can imagine.

In the spiritual world these activities are constantly going on. This is the destination of the pure devotees of the Lord: to interact with the Lord in His eternal pastimes.

1. Brahma-samhita 5.1
2. Bhagavad-gita 4.6

No Loss of Diminution

All material accomplishments are finished at the time of death. "You can't take it with you." The pharaohs in Egypt were buried with their worldly belongings (including their wives and servants), yet thousands of years later their bodies were dug up and all the worldly belongings were still there (unless grave robbers had taken them). We come into this world naked and leave in the same way, regardless of what we have acquired in this lifetime: prestige, money, family, education, etc.

Devotional service performed in this lifetime is never lost. If one becomes 1% Krishna conscious in this lifetime, he will take up devotional service from this point in the next. Krishna informs us that in Krishna consciousness there is no loss or diminution, and that a little Krishna consciousness will protect one from the most dangerous situation--losing the facility of having a human body in the next life.[1]

A devotee who leaves his body after a little devotional service goes to the heavenly planets, and thereafter takes birth in a well-to-do family. During this birth he gets further opportunities to progress in devotional service.[2]

A devotee who leaves his body after a great deal of devotional service takes birth in a family of transcendentalists where he is immediately engaged in devotional service and is able to perfect his Krishna consciousness.[3]

Of course, a devotee who leaves this world after perfecting his devotional service, never comes back to this world again, but attains Krishna's eternal abode, *Goloka Vrindavana.*

1. Bhagavad-gita 2.40
2. Bhagavad-gita 6.41
3. Bhagavad-gita 6.42

No MEAT, FISH, OR EGGS

NO INTOXICATION

NO ILLICIT SEX

NO GAMBLING

The Regulative Principles of Freedom

There are positive and negative injunctions for those wishing to be successful in spiritual life. For example, if one wishes to start a fire he must apply heat (positive injunction) as well as avoid pouring water (negative injunction). If one has a disease and wishes to recover, he must take the medicine (positive injunction) that the doctor prescribes, and avoid certain foods (negative injunction) which would hurt his recovery.

There are four pillars of sinful life: the eating of meat, fish and eggs; the taking of intoxication; the attempt to enjoy illicit sex (sex outside of marriage); and gambling. These activities pollute the consciousness, whereas devotional service purifies the consciousness.

In addition, one who performs these activities will have to suffer a heavy karmic burden. That is, he will have to experience very negative reactions in the future for the activities performed at present.

One normally thinks that regulations are restrictions on freedom, but a little reflection will help one realize that this is not so. When criminal activity is restricted, citizens are "free" to walk on the streets. When one regulates his eating and exercising, one becomes "free" to enjoy healthy life. Likewise, by not engaging in meat-eating, intoxication, illicit sex and gambling, the individual becomes free of their negative effects. His consciousness becomes less restricted by material conditions and bad karma so that he is able to better understand spiritual truths.

One who does not follow these restrictions, is not considered to be truly a human being, even though he may possess a human body.

Service to God

The *Vedic* literatures recognize that each person is an individual, with specific abilities and propensities. A devotee is engaged in Krishna's service in accordance with these proclivities. What makes the activity devotional service is that the results are offered to Krishna.

In the *Bhagavad-gita*, Krishna stresses that all of the results of all of our activities should be offered to Him.[1] The devotee consults the spiritual master to determine which activities are in harmony with his psychophysical nature, and how to offer the results of such activities to the Supreme Lord. The devotee may be engaged in a variety of activities, but in each of them the devotee is thinking of pleasing Krishna and the spiritual master.

Devotional service is open to everyone, regardless of caste, creed, race, or sex. Devotees see beyond the body to the soul, and therefore are free from all material bias. A devotee is never to be considered a man, woman, black, white, or any other designation that pertains to the body. A devotee is simply seen as a servant of God.

1. Bhagavad-gita 9.27

The Six Senses

In the *Bhagavad-gita* Krishna explains that we have six senses, including the mind. At the present time, because we are identifying with the material body, we are controlled by these senses. Depending upon which of the three modes of nature (goodness, passion, and ignorance) we happen to be affected by, we seek certain objects for each of these senses in order to satisfy them (the senses). As one thinks about the sense objects one develops a desire or attachment for them and this desire causes one to attempt to obtain them.[1] However, once obtained, the senses demand more or different sense objects. The person who relies on his senses to obtain knowledge is bewildered since his senses are faulty.

This world is full of variety. Businesses are creating and providing products not only to fulfill all types of desires for sense gratification, but to stimulate new desires with the aid of the mass media. Thus, the living entity is being pulled here and there by his senses in an never-ending attempt to become satisfied.

Only by engaging the senses in the service of God can one be freed from slavery to the senses.

1. Bhagavad-gita 2.62

Controlled Senses

A devotee realizes that the source of his miseries in this world, the senses, can also be the cause of his liberation and perfection in Krishna consciousness. Generally it is thought that sense control means severe austerity or joyless puritanism, but there is no need to negate the senses or ignore the senses in Krishna consciousness. One simply has to engage the senses in Krishna's service, recognizing that Krishna is the proprietor of the senses.

The spiritual master and the *Vedic* literatures guide the devotee in engaging his senses in the Lord's service. When the senses are thus utilized, they regain their original spiritual nature and the devotee can be said to be enjoying them.

If we understand our bodies to be temples of God and our senses to be His property, then we can engage them happily in Krishna's service.

The ears are engaged in hearing about the Lord. The eyes are engaged in seeing the beautiful form of the Lord. The nose can be engaged in smelling the flowers offered to Krishna. The hands (touch) can be engaged in working for Krishna and touching the lotus feet of Krishna and His devotees. The tongue can be engaged in tasting food offered to Krishna, and speaking about Him. Finally, the mind, the sixth sense, can be engaged in thinking of Krishna's names, activities, forms, qualities, and service. All the senses thus become a source of great happiness for a devotee.

A Krishna Conscious Diet

Krishna states in the *Bhagavad-gita* that whatever one eats, one should offer to Him first, before partaking of it.[1] If one neglects this injunction, one is verily eating only sin.[2] This means that there will be a karmic reaction for eating any type of food--even food in the mode of goodness--unless the food is first offered to God as a sacrifice.

Krishna is a person and has personal likes and dislikes. There are certain foods that He considers acceptable, such as fruits, vegetables, grains, and milk products.[3] If we want Krishna to accept our offering, it is necessary to confine ourselves to the groups of foods that He will accept, otherwise the offering will be in vain--He will reject it.

The attitude in which one offers the foodstuffs to Krishna is most important. Krishna states that one should offer the food with "love and devotion". This means that one should make the offering and do the cooking with the idea of preparing the food for the pleasure of Krishna.

A Krishna conscious person prepares the food in a clean place, never tasting the preparations before they are offered. He uses the authorized ingredients. When he is finished with the preparation, he puts a sample of each dish on a special plate that is used only for Krishna's eating. Placing this dish on the altar before Krishna, he prays with devotion for the Lord to accept his humble presentation. After this offering, the plate is cleansed and put away. Then the devotee partakes of the Lord's remnants, and is purified by doing so.

1. Bhagavad-gita 9.27
2. Bhagavad-gita 3.13
3. Bhagavad-gita 9.26

A Higher Taste

People often wonder how a devotee can execute the process of devotional service so faithfully while still being surrounded by so many attractive material features. When Srila Prabhupada's Godbrother was preaching in England to a member of the nobility, he requested the nobleman to follow the four regulative principles: no meat, fish or eggs; no gambling; no illicit sex; and no intoxication. The gentleman replied, "Impossible!"

But a devotee is experiencing such pleasure from the Lord's service, that he considers such material affairs as insignificant. This is called a "higher taste". This material world is a perverted reflection of the spiritual realm. So, when we experience the real thing, there is no more attraction to the reflection.[1]

One, for example, may be attracted to dancing for one's own pleasure, which is certainly material. But, when one experiences dancing for Krishna, he forgets such paltry, dry affairs as material dancing. A devotee chants the holy names of God: **Hare Krishna Hare Krishna Krishna Krishna Hare Hare Hare Rama Hare Rama Rama Rama Hare Hare**, and dances in ecstacy.

Once can eat for Krishna, speak for Krishna, act for Krishna, or practically anything one would do for himself, can be done for Krishna. All the senses can be thus engaged in serving Krishna.

1. Bhagavad-gita 2.59

The Peace Formula

Everyone wants peace and happiness. This is not obtainable materially. If we study history we will not find a single man who has obtained this goal through material means. Unfortunately, we refuse to learn from history, and we obstinately think that this elusive peace will be ours one day.

A fish out of the water can never be happy, regardless of the amenities that it is given to enjoy--furniture, clothes, television, etc. Similarly, the soul, when it is not acting in its constitutional position (servant of God) will always be uncomfortable.

Real peace can be had by accepting the fact that Krishna is the enjoyer, proprietor, beneficiary of all activities, and our eternal well-wisher.[1]

Krishna is the proprietor of all of the planets and universes. No one is greater than Him. He is the master of the material nature, and all living entities are bound by His laws. Fortunately, He is also our greatest friend. So by obeying and serving Him lovingly, we can find true peace and happiness.

1. Bhagavad-gita 5.29

An Invitation

You are invited to attend our weekly open house which is held every Sunday. There are discussions on mantra meditation, karma, reincarnation, and the other topics dealt with in this book. A free sumptuous vegetarian dinner will be served. The program begins at 5:00 P.M. Call for information.

Iskcon of North Carolina
P.O. Box 897
Hillsborough, N.C. 27278
(919) 732-6492

How to get to New Goloka

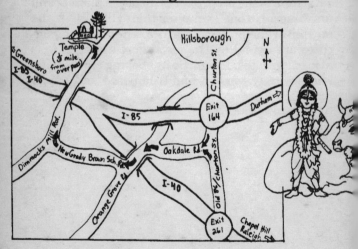

Special thanks for help with the publication of this book to:
Harish Patel
R.T. Bulsara
Thankorbhai Topiwalla